THE Cook's JOURNAL

WITH QUOTATIONS, ILLUSTRATIONS, AND SPACE
FOR RECIPES AND REFLECTION

D1709471

RUNNING PRESS
PHILADELPHIA · LONDON

ABOUT THE ILLUSTRATOR

Christopher Wormell is the author and illustrator of the best-selling children's book, *An Alphabet of Animals*, winner of the Graphics Prize at the Bologna Book Fair in 1990. A self-taught artist who dropped out of school at age 18 to pursue painting, he began engraving in 1982 and has won worldwide recognition as an illustrator. *An Alphabet of Animals* was followed by an illustrated edition of *Mowgli's Brothers*, the first story of Rudyard Kipling's *The Jungle Book*, and *A Number of Animals*, which was featured on *The New York Times* list of books of the year.

Copyright © 1994 by Running Press.
Illustrations copyright © 1994 by Christopher Wormell.

Canadian representatives: General Publishing Co., Ltd., 30 Lesmill Road, Don Mills, Ontario M3B 2T6.

9 8 7 6 5 4 3 2 1
Digit on the right indicates the number of this printing.

ISBN 1–56138–423–2

Cover design by E. June Roberts
Cover and interior illustrations by Christopher Wormell
Interior design by Lili Schwartz
Edited by Melissa Stein
Typography: Copperplate and MT Centaur by Deborah Lugar
Printed in Hong Kong

This book may be ordered by mail from the publisher.
Please add $2.50 for postage and handling.
But try your bookstore first!

Running Press Book Publishers, 125 South Twenty-second Street, Philadelphia, Pennsylvania 19103–4399

The Cook's Journal

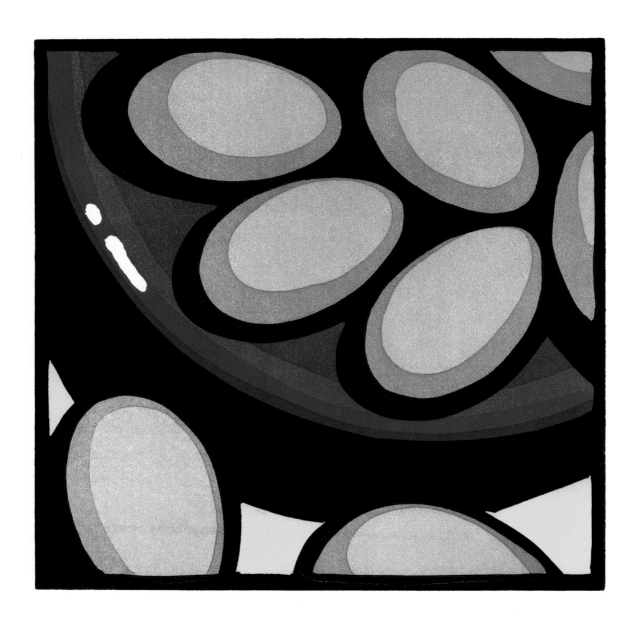

AN EGG IS ALWAYS AN
ADVENTURE.

Oscar Wilde (1854–1900)
Irish poet and playwright

FOR THOSE WHO LOVE
IT, COOKING IS AT ONCE
CHILD'S PLAY AND ADULT
JOY. AND COOKING DONE
WITH CARE IS AN ACT
OF LOVE.

Craig Claiborne, b. 1920
American writer

WHAT WAS PARADISE,
BUT A GARDEN FULL OF
VEGETABLES AND HERBS
AND PLEASURE? NOTHING
THERE BUT DELIGHTS.

William Lawson
17th-century writer

First parents of the human race, whose
gourmandism is historical, you lost all for
an apple, what would you not have done for a
truffled turkey?

Anthelme Brillat-Savarin (1775–1826)
French politician and writer

GOOD FOOD HAS A MAGIC APPEAL. YOU MAY GROW
OLD, EVEN UGLY, BUT IF YOU ARE A GOOD COOK,
PEOPLE WILL ALWAYS FIND THE PATH TO YOUR DOOR.

James Beard (1903–1985)
American chef and writer

OUR OWN FOOD WAS GOOD, SIMPLE GOOD. PASTA
MADE AT HOME, CLEAR LEAN BROTH DISTILLED FROM
A SCRAP OF BEEF AND A BARNYARD FOWL, VEGETABLES
PICKED OUT IN THE MARKET IN THE MORNING AND
OLIVE OIL, IN THOSE FRAGILE GREEN PHIALS BLOWN
AT MURANO, ALWAYS ON THE TABLE. . . .

Sybille Bedford, b. 1911
German-born English writer

I KNOW THE LOOK OF AN APPLE THAT IS ROASTING AND SIZZLING ON THE HEARTH ON A WINTER'S EVENING, AND I KNOW THE COMFORT THAT COMES OF EATING IT HOT, ALONG WITH SOME SUGAR AND A DRENCH OF CREAM. . . . I KNOW HOW THE NUTS TAKEN IN CONJUNCTION WITH WINTER APPLES, CIDER, AND DOUGHNUTS, MAKE OLD PEOPLE'S TALES AND OLD JOKES SOUND FRESH AND CRISP AND ENCHANTING.

Mark Twain (1835–1910)
American writer

. . . SWEET CORN . . . WHAT PLEASURE IT WOULD BE TO PLUNK EARS OF CORN FROM THEIR STALKS AND HURRY THEM SHRIEKING TO THE POT OF BOILING WATER DESTINED FOR THEM. . . . TEN MINUTES IN BOILING WATER ARE ENOUGH, BUT NOT TOO MUCH. THEN BUTTER AND SALT ON THREE ROWS AT A TIME—NOT TWO, WHICH IS CHILDISH; NOT FOUR, WHICH IS GLUTTONOUS—AND THE THREE ROWS EATEN STEADILY FROM LEFT TO RIGHT AS ONE READS POETRY.

Carl Van Doren (1885–1950)
American writer and editor

LET THE SALAD-MAKER BE A SPENDTHRIFT FOR OIL,
A MISER FOR VINEGAR, A STATESMAN FOR SALT,
AND A MADMAN FOR MIXING.

Spanish proverb

LETTUCE, LIKE CONVERSATION, REQUIRES A GOOD
DEAL OF OIL, TO AVOID FRICTION, AND KEEP THE
COMPANY SMOOTH. . . . YOU CAN PUT ANYTHING,
AND THE MORE THINGS THE BETTER, INTO SALAD,
AS INTO A CONVERSATION, BUT EVERYTHING
DEPENDS UPON THE SKILL OF MIXING.

Charles Dudley Warner (1829–1900)
American editor and writer

FRESHNESS, COLOR,
CRISP AND CRUNCHY
TEXTURES, A SENSE
OF SHARING NATURE'S
VITALITY—THEY ARE
ALL WRAPPED UP
IN VEGETABLES.

Miriam Polunin
20th-century American writer,
broadcaster, and editor

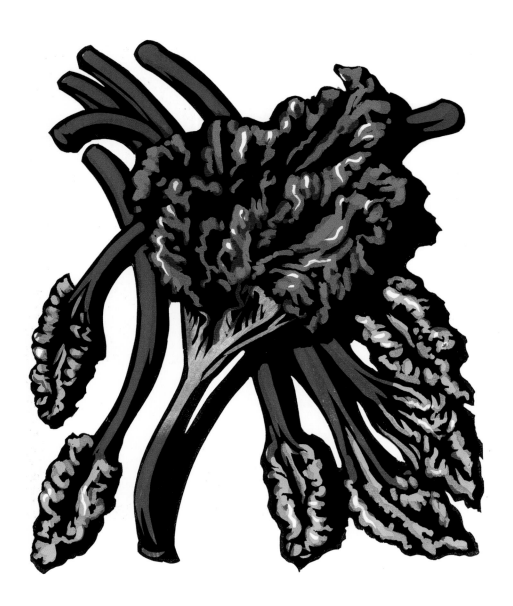

AND MR. ALDERMAN PTOLEMY TORTOISE BROUGHT A
SALAD WITH HIM IN A STRING BAG. AND INSTEAD OF
A NICE DISH OF MINNOWS, THEY HAD A ROASTED
GRASSHOPPER WITH LADY-BIRD SAUCE, WHICH
FROGS CONSIDER A BEAUTIFUL TREAT. . . .

Beatrix Potter (1886–1943)
English writer and illustrator

A SALAD IS NOT A MEAL. IT IS A STYLE.

Fran Lebowitz
20th-century American writer

I HAVE FRIENDS WHO BEGIN WITH PASTA, AND
FRIENDS WHO BEGIN WITH RICE, BUT WHENEVER I
FALL IN LOVE, I BEGIN WITH POTATOES. . . . I HAVE
MADE A LOT OF MISTAKES FALLING IN LOVE, AND
REGRETTED MOST OF THEM, BUT NEVER THE
POTATOES THAT WENT WITH THEM.

Nora Ephron, b. 1941
American writer

POTATO: BLAND, AMIABLE AND HOMELY, AN HONEST
VEGETABLE, GIVING HONOR WHERE HONOR IS DUE—
IN AN HONEST SOUP.

Della Lutes
20th-century American chef

TO MAKE A GOOD SOUP,
THE POT MUST ONLY
SIMMER OR "SMILE."

French proverb

BEAUTIFUL SOUP! WHO CARES FOR FISH,
GAME, OR ANY OTHER DISH?
WHO WOULD NOT GIVE ALL ELSE FOR TWO
PENNYWORTH ONLY OF BEAUTIFUL SOUP?

Lewis Carroll (1832–1898)
English writer and mathematician

I LIVE ON GOOD SOUP,

NOT ON FINE WORDS.

Jean Baptiste Molière (1622–1673)
French actor and playwright

GARLIC, THE INCENSE OF
HOME, THE AROMA OF
FAMILY HAPPINESS.

Linda Casdan, b. 1942
American writer

. . . I'VE DISCOVERED SOMETHING: IF I GIVE THE DISH
A NAME, OR TRANSLATE THE REPULSIVE NAME IT
ALREADY HAS INTO FRENCH, MY FAMILY CAN'T TELL
MY CHEAP CONCOCTION FROM GOURMET FARE.

I HAVE DECIDED THAT THE KEY TO SUCCESSFUL
FOOD PRESENTATION IS ARROGANCE.

Linda Henley, b. 1951
American writer

WHEN MY MOTHER HAD TO
GET DINNER FOR EIGHT
SHE'D JUST MAKE ENOUGH
FOR SIXTEEN AND ONLY
SERVE HALF.

Gracie Allen (1895–1964)
American comedian

JUST AS NO TWO PIECES
OF CREATIVE WORK ARE
ALIKE, SO THE SAME DISH
PREPARED BY DIFFERENT
COOKS EXHIBITS AS MANY
INDIVIDUALIZED FLAVORS
AS IT HAS INTERPRETERS.

Julie Sahni, b. 1945
Indian chef

. . . A RECIPE IS ONLY
A THEME, WHICH AN
INTELLIGENT COOK CAN
PLAY EACH TIME WITH
VARIATION.

Jehane Benoît (1904–1987)
Canadian chef

ULTIMATELY, YOUR
SEASONINGS WILL
BECOME A PART OF THE
DISH, THE WAY A
PERFUME BECOMES A
PART OF AN INDIVIDUAL.

Paul Prudhomme, b. 1940
American chef

SOMETIMES . . . IT TAKES
ME AN ENTIRE DAY TO
WRITE A RECIPE, TO
COMMUNICATE IT
CORRECTLY. IT'S REALLY
LIKE WRITING A LITTLE
SHORT STORY. . . .

Julia Child, b. 1912
American chef

I BELIEVE THAT THE TRULY DEDICATED COOK HAS
FOOD IN HER MIND, OR AT LEAST ON THE PERIPHERY
OF IT, AT ALL TIMES. AS A POET UNCONSCIOUSLY
EARMARKS A WORD THAT RHYMES HANDILY WITH
ANOTHER, OR AS A PAINTER MENTALLY NOTES A TINT
OF A SHADE OF A COLOR THAT SPELLS DAWN, SO THE
FOOD-MINDED PERSON SNIFFS AN OUT-OF-THE-WAY
HERB, LIKE COSTMARY, AND THINKS IN A FLASH,
BRAISED MOOSE HOCKS!

Peg Bracken, b. 1920
American writer

. . . THE PREPARATION OF GOOD FOOD IS MERELY
ANOTHER EXPRESSION OF ART, ONE OF THE
JOYS OF CIVILIZED LIVING. . . .

Dione Lucas (1909–1971)
English-born American chef

EATING SOMETHING WELL
CONCEIVED AND WELL
MADE IS ONE OF LIFE'S
VERY GREAT PLEASURES.

Simone Beck, b. 1905
Normandy-born French chef

WHAT IS LITERATURE COMPARED WITH COOKING?
THE ONE IS SHADOW, THE OTHER IS SUBSTANCE.

E. V. Lucas (1868–1938)
English writer and publisher

WHEN YOU HAVE HELPED TO RAISE THE STANDARD OF COOKING, YOU HAVE HELPED TO RAISE THE ONLY THING IN THE WORLD THAT REALLY MATTERS ANYHOW. WE ONLY HAVE ONE OR TWO WARS IN A LIFETIME BUT WE HAVE THREE MEALS A DAY.

Will Rogers (1879–1935)
American writer, actor, and humorist

THINK OF THE FOOD YOU ARE ABOUT TO SERVE AS A
STILL LIFE, THE PLATE BEING THE CANVAS AND THE
FOOD ON IT THE PICTURE THAT IS BEING PAINTED.

Holly Garrison
20th-century American writer

MANY EXCELLENT COOKS
ARE SPOILED BY GOING
INTO THE ARTS.

Paul Gauguin (1848–1903)
French artist

MORE PASTA AND
LESS PANACHE.

Mario Puzo, b. 1920
Italian-American writer

**NO MAN IS LONELY WHILE
EATING SPAGHETTI.**

Robert Morley, b. 1908
British actor

He who enters paradise through a door is not a Neopolitan. We make our entrance into that heavenly abode by delicately parting a curtain of spaghetti. As soon as we get weaned from our mother's breast we are fed a fragment of spaghetti. . . . What better inheritance can I leave my sons than spaghetti?

Giuseppe Marotta
20th-century Italian writer

THERE IS NO LOVE
SINCERER THAN THE
LOVE OF FOOD.

George Bernard Shaw (1856–1950)
British playwright

**HUNGER IS THE BEST
SEASONING.**

Ken Follett, b. 1949
English writer

. . . I LOOK UPON IT, THAT
HE WHO DOES NOT MIND
HIS BELLY WILL HARDLY
MIND ANYTHING ELSE.

Samuel Johnson (1709–1784)
English lexicographer and writer

A MAN MAY BE A
PESSIMISTIC DETERMINIST
BEFORE LUNCH AND AN
OPTIMISTIC BELIEVER IN
THE WILL'S FREEDOM
AFTER IT.

Aldous Huxley (1894–1963)
English writer

IT IS HARDER TO BE
UNHAPPY WHEN YOU
ARE EATING.

Kurt Vonnegut, Jr.
20th-century American writer

A LITTLE COOKING IS
GOOD BECAUSE IT
UNSETTLES THE MEAT'S
MIND AND PREPARES IT
FOR NEW IDEAS.

Samuel Butler (1835–1902)
English writer

THE CHANGING OF COLOR
OF A ROAST AS IT TURNS
ON A SPIT IS A THING OF
ENDLESS WONDER,
ENTICING AS A SUNSET.

Craig Claiborne, b. 1920
American writer

"ROAST BEEF MEDIUM"
IS NOT A FOOD. IT IS
A PHILOSOPHY.

Edna Ferber (1887–1968)
American writer

I AM NOT A GLUTTONOUS EATER, YOU UNDERSTAND,
BUT A CONSTANT ONE WHO THINKS OF A FAST AS
THREE HOURS WITHOUT FOOD. THIS IS BECAUSE I
WAS RAISED ON WINNIE THE POOH WHO WAS, IN
TURN, RAISED ON DEMAND FEEDING. HIS INTERNAL
CLOCK DIDN'T REGISTER LUNCH TIME OR DINNER
TIME BUT RATHER, "TIME FOR A LITTLE SOMETHING."

Ellen Goodman, b. 1941
American writer and journalist

WHAT I SAY IS THAT
IF A MAN REALLY LIKES
POTATOES, HE MUST BE
A PRETTY DECENT SORT
OF FELLOW.

A. A. Milne (1882–1956)
English writer

WE FIND OF THOSE BOUNTIES
WHICH HEAVEN DOES GIVE,
THAT SOME LIVE TO EAT,
AND THAT SOME EAT TO LIVE. . . .

19th-century Shaker saying

. . . APPETITE TURNS
COMMON FOOD INTO THE
FARE OF KINGS.

Laurel Lee
20th-century American writer

HAD I BUT ONE PENNY IN THE WORLD,
THOU SHOULDST HAVE IT FOR GINGERBREAD.

William Shakespeare (1561–1616)
English playwright and poet

ONE OF THE DELIGHTS
OF LIFE IS EATING WITH
FRIENDS; SECOND TO THAT
IS TALKING ABOUT
EATING.

Laurie Colwin (1944–1992)
American writer

THE ART OF COOKING
PRODUCES THE DISHES,
BUT IT IS THE ART OF
EATING THAT TRANS-
FORMS THEM INTO
A MEAL.

Marcella Hazan, b. 1924
Italian-born American writer

SOUR CREAM, YUM! BREAK PIECES OF BREAD INTO
IT. SOUR CREAM WITH FARMER-CHEESE. MMM! SOUR
CREAM WITH EGGS. SOUR CREAM WITH WHAT ELSE?
BORSCHT . . . STRAWBERRIES . . . RADISHES . . .
BANANAS. . . .

Henry Roth, b. 1906
American writer

WITH BREAD ALL
SORROWS ARE LESS.

Miguel de Cervantes (1547–1616)
Spanish writer

GOOD BREAD IS THE MOST FUNDAMENTALLY
SATISFYING OF ALL FOODS; AND GOOD BREAD WITH
FRESH BUTTER, THE GREATEST OF FEASTS.

James Beard (1903–1985)
American chef and writer

. . . GOOD SOURDOUGH

. . . GOES ON FOREVER.

James Michener, b. 1907
American writer

WORKING DOUGH.
WORKING, WORKING
DOUGH. NOTHING BETTER
THAN THAT TO START THE
DAY'S SERIOUS WORK OF
BEATING BACK THE PAST.

Toni Morrison, b. 1931
African-American writer

FOOD FRAGRANCES . . . LINGER IN MEMORY MORE
STRONGLY THAN TASTES. . . . OVEN-FRESH BREAD
SPREAD WITH BUTTER AND HOMEMADE BERRY JAM
. . . BOWLS OF STEAMING VEGETABLE-BEEF SCENTED
SOUP ALONG WITH HOT CORN BREAD FOR SUPPER
ON EVENINGS WHEN RAIN SPLASHED AGAINST
WINDOWPANES . . . WARM SUGARY-CINNAMON ROLLS
BROUGHT OVER BY A NEIGHBOR . . . THERE'S
NOTHING LIKE THE AROMA OF YEAST BREAD. . . .

Nell B. Nichols
20th-century food editor

WHEN THERE IS VERY LITTLE ELSE LEFT TO BELIEVE
IN, ONE CAN STILL BELIEVE IN AN HONEST LOAF OF
FRAGRANT, HOME-BAKED BREAD.

Anna Thomas, b. 1948
German chef and writer

WHAT I LOVE ABOUT COOKING IS THAT AFTER A HARD DAY, THERE IS SOMETHING COMFORTING ABOUT THE FACT THAT IF YOU MELT BUTTER AND ADD FLOUR AND THEN HOT STOCK, IT WILL GET THICK! . . . IT'S A SURE THING IN A WORLD WHERE NOTHING IS SURE. . . .

Nora Ephron, b. 1941
American writer

THERE IS A CERTAIN SYMPATICO BETWEEN AUTUMN
AND STOCK-MAKING. PERHAPS IT IS THE PERVASIVE
AROMA THAT FOGS THE KITCHEN WINDOWS AS THE
BROTH SIMMERS AND THICKENS, IMBUING A HOME
WITH A SENSE OF WELL-BEING.

Molly O'Neill
20th-century American writer

AN UNWATCHED POT

BOILS IMMEDIATELY.

H. F. Ellis, b. 1907
English writer

IF YOU'RE IN A HURRY,
JUST EAT YOUR SANDWICH
AND GO. DON'T EVEN
START COOKING, BECAUSE
YOU CAN'T DO ANYTHING
WELL IN A HURRY.

Leah Chase
20th-century American chef

GOOD COOKING IS THE
FOOD OF A PURE
CONSCIENCE.

Desessarts [Denis Dechanel] (1738–1793)
French actor and gastronome

SOUP AND FISH EXPLAIN
HALF THE EMOTIONS
OF LIFE.

Sydney Smith (1771–1845)
English clergyman and essayist

FISH, TO TASTE RIGHT,
MUST SWIM THREE
TIMES—IN WATER, IN
BUTTER, AND IN WINE.

Polish proverb

I LIKE A COOK WHO
SMILES OUT LOUD WHEN
HE TASTES HIS OWN
WORK.

Robert Farrar Capon, b. 1925
American priest, writer, and chef

EGGS OF AN HOUR,
BREAD OF A DAY, WINE
OF A YEAR, A FRIEND
OF THIRTY YEARS.

Italian proverb

A MEAL WITHOUT WINE
IS LIKE A DAY WITHOUT
SUNSHINE.

Anthelme Brillat-Savarin
(1755–1826)
French politician and writer

TOO MANY COOKS MAY
SPOIL THE BROTH, BUT
IT ONLY TAKES ONE TO
BURN IT.

Madeleine Bingham, b. 1912
American writer

YOU CAN'T MAKE SOUFFLÉ
RISE TWICE.

Alice Roosevelt Longworth (1884–1980)
American hostess

. . . IT TAKES MORE THAN INGREDIENTS AND
TECHNIQUE TO COOK A GOOD MEAL. A GOOD
COOK PUTS SOMETHING OF HIMSELF INTO THE
PREPARATION—HE COOKS WITH ENJOYMENT,
ANTICIPATION, SPONTANEITY, AND HE IS
WILLING TO EXPERIMENT.

Pearl Bailey (1918–1990)
American singer

COOKING IS LIKE LOVE. IT SHOULD BE ENTERED INTO
WITH ABANDON OR NOT AT ALL.

Harriet Van Horne, b. 1920
American newspaper columnist and critic

THE PERSON WHO
PRODUCED THIS KIND OF
SMELL REALLY KNEW HOW
TO COOK.

Laura Esquirel, b. 1950
Mexican writer

GARLIC IS MUSICAL IN ITS
ABILITY TO CREATE A
LIVELY YET DEEP
REGISTER ON THE PALATE.

Lloyd Harris, b. 1947
American writer

THE HERBS AND SPICES ARE THE WINDOWS:
THEY LET IN THE SUNSHINE.

Paul Prudhomme, b. 1940
American chef

IF THE DEFINITION OF POETRY ALLOWED THAT IT
COULD BE COMPOSED WITH THE PRODUCTS OF THE
FIELD AS WELL AS WITH WORDS, PESTO WOULD BE
IN EVERY ANTHOLOGY.

Marcella Hazan, b. 1924
Italian-born American writer

GARLIC, LIKE MAKEUP, SHOULD NEVER BE OBVIOUS.

Adele Davis (1904–1974)
American nutritionist and writer

THERE IS NO SUCH THING

AS A LITTLE GARLIC.

Arthur Baer (1886–1969)
American journalist

SALT IS WHITE AND
PURE—THERE IS
SOMETHING HOLY IN SALT.

Nathaniel Hawthorne (1804–1864)
American writer

TO TAKE PARSLEY AWAY FROM THE COOK WOULD
MAKE IT ALMOST IMPOSSIBLE FOR HIM TO EXERCISE
HIS ART.

Louis Bose d'Antic
18th-century French writer

THE WORLD WOULD NOT BE THE SAME WITHOUT
CHILES: SWEET, OR HOT, OR JUST SUPPORTIVE. . . .
AT ONCE STARKLY THERMAL, ELEGANTLY FINISHING,
FRESH, RESTORATIVE, BANG-ON CHEMICALLY
HEALTHY, SUPERDIGESTIVE, AND QUITE BEAUTIFUL
AS OBJECTS IN THEMSELVES.

Richard Condon, b. 1915
American writer

IT IS HARD TO SAY WHAT IT IS ABOUT CHILIES THAT CAUSES AN ADDICTION. PERHAPS IT IS THE EXQUISITE PAIN THEY BRING THAT HEIGHTENS THE PLEASURE OF EATING, BUT ONCE YOU HAVE ENJOYED THEM, THERE IS NO TURNING BACK: YOU ARE HOOKED FOREVER.

Madhur Jaffrey
20th-century Indian chef

ALL ANIMALS FEED,
BUT ONLY HUMAN BEINGS
SAVOR FOOD WITH SUCH
PASSION.

Robert Crastein, b. 1942
Psychologist and brain researcher

THE FLAVOR OF FRYING
BACON BEATS ORANGE
BLOSSOMS.

P. Benjamin (1811–1884)
American Confederate statesman

THE SIZZLE OF BACON,
THE FIZZ OF CHAMPAGNE,
THE SOUND OF LAUGHTER
AT A PARTY—OUR EARS
ARE CONSTANTLY TUNED
TO THE SNAP, CRACKLE
AND POP OF THE GASTRO-
NOMIC EXPERIENCE.

William J. Garry, b. 1944
American editor

PRESERVE SUMMER IN
GLASS JARS. MAKE JAM.

Helen Simpson
20th-century English writer

. . . ORANGES . . . THE TASTE EQUIVALENT OF GOLD.

Alice Walker, b. 1944
African-American writer

ON STRAWBERRIES:
DOUBTLESS GOD COULD
HAVE MADE A BETTER
BERRY, BUT DOUBTLESS
GOD NEVER DID.

William Butler Yeats (1865–1939)
Irish poet and playwright

... BLACKBERRIES ...
TASTING SO GOOD AND
HAPPY THAT TO EAT THEM
WAS LIKE BEING IN
CHURCH.

Toni Morrison, b. 1931
African-American writer

A PERFECTLY RIPE PEACH
IS WORTH WAITING FOR
ALL SUMMER LONG.

Julee Rosso and Sheila Lukins
20th-century American food editors

GIVE ME BOOKS, FRUIT,
FRENCH WINE AND FINE
WEATHER, AND A LITTLE
MUSIC OUT OF DOORS,
PLAYED BY SOMEONE I
DO NOT KNOW.

John Keats (1795–1821)
English poet

SUMMER COOKING IMPLIES A SENSE OF IMMEDIACY,
A CAPACITY TO CAPTURE THE ESSENCE OF THE
FLEETING MOMENT.

Elizabeth David
20th-century English writer

. . . ALL EXQUISITE CREATIONS ARE SHORT-LIVED.
THE NATURAL TERM OF AN APPLE-PIE IS BUT
TWELVE HOURS.

Henry Ward Beecher (1813–1887)
American minister and editor

THE POMEGRANATE IS NATURE'S LITTLE TEASE,
INVITING YOU TO GUESS WHICH PARTS OF IT ARE
EDIBLE AND WHICH ARE NOT. SOME PEOPLE THROW
OUT THE SEEDS AND ARE SORRY AFTERWARDS,
AND SOME PEOPLE EAT THE PULP AND ARE SORRY
ABOUT THAT.

Judith Martin, b. 1938
American writer

[SUGAR IS] THE ROOT
OF GREAT EVIL. GIVE
CHILDREN HONEY
INSTEAD.

Marlene Dietrich (1901–1992)
German-born American actress

WHEN ONE HAS TASTED WATERMELONS ONE KNOWS
WHAT ANGELS EAT.

Mark Twain (1835–1910)
American writer

**THE GREATEST DISHES
ARE VERY SIMPLE DISHES.**

Auguste Escoffier (1847–1935)
French chef and writer

EVEN AT ELEVEN, THEY SAY SHE COULD MAKE THE MOST DELICIOUS BISCUITS AND GRAVY, COBBLER, FRIED CHICKEN, TURNIP GREENS, AND BLACK-EYED PEAS. AND HER DUMPLINGS WERE SO LIGHT THEY WOULD FLOAT IN THE AIR AND YOU'D HAVE TO CATCH 'EM TO EAT 'EM.

Fannie Flagg, b. 1941
American actress and writer

MY GRANDMOTHER COOKS FOR HOURS EACH DAY. . . .
I WOKE UP AT SIX ONE MORNING LAST WEEK AND
SMELLED A THICK, SWEET CHOCOLATE WAFTING UP
FROM THE KITCHEN. . . . A RICH, FRENCH CRÈME
CAKE AT THE BREAK OF DAWN. . . . IT'S A LITTLE LIKE
HAVING BRANDY WITH YOUR CEREAL. I AM OF THE
OPINION THAT OTHER THAN KISSING, ANYTHING
FRENCH SHOULD BE SAVED FOR LATER IN THE DAY.

Renée Manfredi
20th-century American writer

EPICURE: ONE WHO GETS
NOTHING BETTER THAN
THE CREAM OF EVERY-
THING BUT CHEERFULLY
MAKES THE BEST OF IT.

Oliver Hereford (1863–1935)
American humorist

SERENELY FULL, THE EPICURE WOULD SAY,
FATE CANNOT HARM ME, I HAVE DINED TODAY.

Sydney Smith (1771–1845)
English clergyman and essayist

A GOURMET CAN TELL
FROM THE FLAVOR
WHETHER A WOODCOCK'S
LEG IS THE ONE ON WHICH
THE BIRD IS ACCUSTOMED
TO ROOST.

Lucius Beebe (1902–1966)
American journalist

COOKERY IS MY ONE
VANITY AND I AM A
SLAVE TO ANY GUEST
WHO PRAISES MY
CULINARY ART.

Marjorie Kinnan Rawlings (1896–1953)
American writer

A GOOD COOK IS HALF A PHYSICIAN.

Andrew Boorde (1490?–1549)
English Doctor of Physick

THE LAST MAN IN THE
WORLD WHOSE OPINION I
WOULD TAKE ON WHAT TO
EAT WOULD BE A DOCTOR. IT
IS FAR SAFER TO CONSULT
A WAITER, AND NOT A BIT
MORE EXPENSIVE.

Robert Lynd (1879–1949)
Anglo-Irish essayist and journalist

[COOKING] CALLS FOR A LIGHT HEAD, A GENEROUS
SPIRIT, AND A LARGE HEART.

Paul Gauguin (1848–1903)
French artist

"A Jug of Wine, A Loaf of Bread—and
Thou"—what better prescription for a
loving afternoon?

Barbara Kafka
20th-century American writer

KISSING DON'T LAST;
COOKERY DO!

George Meredith (1828–1909)
English writer

MEAT AND POTATOES
ARE ALL YE KNOW ON
EARTH, AND ALL YE
NEED TO KNOW.
THE REST IS GRAVY.

Chris Maynard and William Scheller
20th-century writers

MAN IS A COOKING ANIMAL. THE BEASTS HAVE
MEMORY, JUDGMENT, AND ALL THE FACULTIES AND
PASSIONS OF OUR MIND, IN A CERTAIN DEGREE;
BUT NO BEAST IS A COOK.

James Boswell (1740–1795)
Scottish writer and lawyer

THERE IS A COMMUNION
OF MORE THAN OUR
BODIES WHEN BREAD
IS BROKEN AND WINE
IS DRUNK.

Mary Frances Kennedy Fisher (1908–1992)
American writer

MY KITCHEN IS A MYSTICAL PLACE, A KIND OF
TEMPLE FOR ME. IT IS A PLACE WHERE THE SUR-
FACES SEEM TO HAVE SIGNIFICANCE, WHERE THE
SOUNDS AND ODORS CARRY MEANING THAT
TRANSFERS FROM THE PAST AND BRIDGES
TO THE FUTURE.

Pearl Bailey (1918–1990)
American singer

A LOT OF POETRY OF LIVING, ESPECIALLY ALONE,
TAKES PLACE IN THE KITCHEN.

Charlotte Zolotov, b. 1915
American writer

WHOEVER TELLS A LIE CANNOT BE PURE IN
HEART, AND ONLY THE PURE IN HEART CAN MAKE
A GOOD SOUP.

Ludwig van Beethoven (1770–1827)
German composer

. . . MY KITCHEN IS WHERE EVERYBODY
CONGREGATES, FOR HUMAN BEINGS ARE HEAT-
SEEKING CREATURES, AND THE KITCHEN IS THE
HEARTH. IF A HOUSE CAN BE COMPARED TO A BODY,
THE KITCHEN IS THE HEART OF THE MATTER.

Phyllis Theroux, b. 1939
American writer

THE GLOWING HEARTH SHOOTS BEAMS OF LIGHT
INTO ALL CORNERS, CUTS OUT GREAT SHADOWS
ON THE CEILING, CASTS A FRESH ROSE TINT ON THE
BLUE FAIENCE, AND MAKES THE FANTASTIC
EDIFICE OF PANS GLOW LIKE A WALL OF FIRE. . . .
"THIS KITCHEN IS A WORLD AND THIS CHIMNEY IS
THE SUN."

Victor Hugo (1802–1885)
French writer and poet

IN MY IDEAL COUNTRY KITCHEN, MY LOAVES OF
BREAD ARE AS ROUND AND CIRCULAR AS THE
SEASONS OF THE YEAR AND THE PATH OF PLANETS
AND STARS THAT ORDER MY LIFE. . . .

Betty Fussell
20th-century American writer

. . . ALL FOOD IS A GIFT OF THE GODS AND HAS
SOMETHING OF THE MIRACULOUS; THE EGG NO LESS
THAN THE TRUFFLE.

Sybille Bedford, b. 1911
English writer

GIVE US THIS DAY OUR DAILY TASTE. RESTORE TO US
SOUPS THAT SPOONS WILL NOT SINK IN AND SAUCES
WHICH ARE NEVER THE SAME TWICE. RAISE UP
AMONG US STEWS WITH MORE GRAVY THAN WE HAVE
BREAD TO BLOT IT WITH. . . . GIVE US PASTA WITH
A HUNDRED FILLINGS.

Robert Farrar Capon, b. 1925
American priest, writer, and chef

DO YOU HAVE A KINDER, MORE ADAPTABLE FRIEND IN THE FOOD WORLD THAN SOUP? WHO SOOTHES YOU WHEN YOU ARE ILL? WHO REFUSES TO LEAVE YOU WHEN YOU ARE IMPOVERISHED AND STRETCHES ITS RESOURCES TO GIVE YOU HEARTY SUSTENANCE AND CHEER? WHO WARMS YOU IN WINTER AND COOLS YOU IN SUMMER? YET WHO IS ALSO CAPABLE OF DOING HONOR TO YOUR RICHEST TABLE AND IMPRESSING YOUR MOST DEMANDING GUESTS?

Judith Martin, b. 1938
American writer

MAKE THE EGG AN
AMICABLE MEDIATOR
WHO COMES BETWEEN
DIFFERENT PARTS OF
FOOD TO BRING
ABOUT DIFFICULT
RECONCILIATION.

Desessarts [Denis Dechanel]
(1738–1793)
French actor and gastronome

THE DISCOVERY OF A NEW
DISH DOES MORE FOR THE
HAPPINESS OF THE
HUMAN RACE THAN THE
DISCOVERY OF A STAR.

Anthelme Brillat-Savarin
(1775–1826)
French politician and writer